SandCastle 2

More Blends

ght

Pam Scheunemann

ABDO Publishing Company

Published by SandCastle™, an imprint of ABDO Publishing Company, 8000 West 78th Street, Edina, Minnesota 55439.

Printed in the United States of America, North Mankato, Minnesota.

Cover and interior photo credits: Comstock, Corbis Images, Corel, Digital Vision, PhotoDisc, Rubberball Productions

Library of Congress Cataloging-in-Publication Data

Scheunemann, Pam, 1955-
    Ght / Pam Scheunemann.
      p. cm. -- (Blends)
    Includes index.
    ISBN 1-57765-449-8 (hardcover)
    ISBN 1-59197-038-5 (paperback)
    ISBN 13 978-1-57765-449-0 (hardcover)

    1. Readers (Primary) [1. Readers.] I. Title. II. Blends (Series)

PE1119 .S4315 2001
428.1--dc21
                                                              00-056565

The SandCastle concept, content, and reading method have been reviewed and approved by a national advisory board including literacy specialists, librarians, elementary school teachers, early childhood education professionals, and parents.

Let Us Know

After reading the book, SandCastle would like you to tell us your stories about reading. What is your favorite page? Was there something hard that you needed help with? Share the ups and downs of learning to read. We want to hear from you! To get posted on the ABDO Publishing Company Web site, send us email at:

sandcastle@abdopub.com

About SandCastle™

A professional team of educators, reading specialists, and content developers created the SandCastle™ series to support young readers as they develop reading skills and strategies and increase their general knowledge. The SandCastle™ series has four levels that correspond to early literacy development in young children. The levels are provided to help teachers and parents select the appropriate books for young readers.

Emerging Readers
(no flags)

Beginning Readers
(1 flag)

Transitional Readers
(2 flags)

Fluent Readers
(3 flags)

These levels are meant only as a guide. All levels are subject to change.

ABDO
Publishing Company

ght

Brighton caught some fish.

He thought it was fun.

ght

Amy is thoughtful.

She bought Mrs. Knight the right gift.

ght

Leighton runs to put
his kite in flight.

ght

Amanda loves the sight of bright blue flowers.

ght

My friend Dwight is mighty bright.

We never fight.

ght

This mom holds her daughter tight.

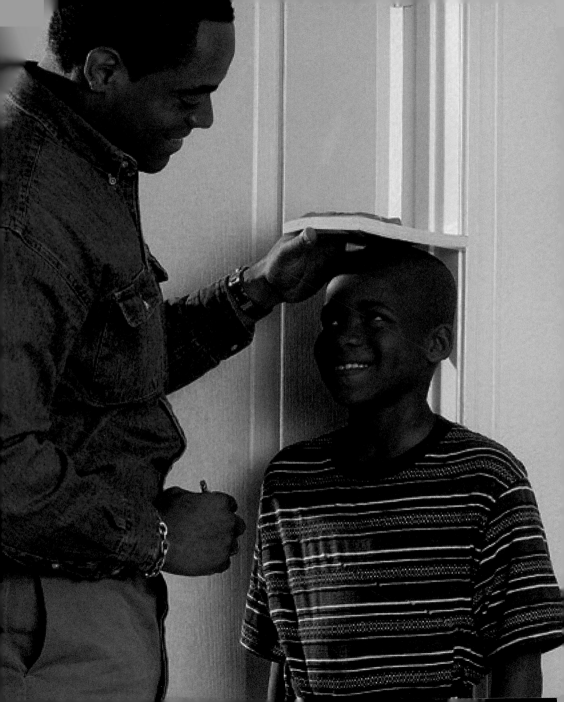

ght

Steven is the height
and weight he ought
to be.

17

ght

My Grandpa Wright is eighty years old.